Donated By
Columbia Lodge
B'nai B'rith Men
#2889

Howard County Jewish Community School, Inc.
The Meeting House
5885 Robert Oliver Place
Columbia, Maryland 21045

by Norma Simon

illustrations by Ayala Gordon

United Synagogue Commission on Jewish Education

Copyright © 1959 by United Synagogue of America · Printed in U.S.A.
Second Printing 1976

Fall is full of holidays
> for David and for me,
>> for Mother and for Daddy,
>>> and for all the Jewish people.
After the High Holidays,
> Daddy tells us a story.

Daddy always begins,
"Once upon a time,

The Jewish people were on their way,
a long, long way to *Eretz Yisrael*.
It took a long, long time to get there,
walking and walking the long, long way.

"They were going to make a new home
    in a new place to live,
    where their children could grow up,
    where they could build houses,
    where they could settle down
    for a long, long time.

"On their long, long way
   they stopped in many places.
They built huts,   very small houses.
They made the huts out of things
   they could find,
   huts like our *Sukkah*,
   to live in a little while.

"Their huts were not very cozy,
and not very big,
and not a real home.

"After a long, long time,
    and many different places,
        and many different huts,

the Jewish people came to *Eretz Yisrael,*
    a place where they could build,
    a place where they could pray,
    a place where they could stay
    for a long, long time.

"This is why we build a *Sukkah*,
   a little house to stand for 9 days,
   to remember that once upon a time
   the Jewish people lived in huts,
   on their way to *Eretz Yisrael*."

Daddy tells us about his *Sukkah,*
 the *Sukkah* his father built,
 when Daddy was a little boy.

Every year I say to Daddy,
 "This year,   for the first time,
   let's build our very own *Sukkah,*
    just for us and Grandma and Grandpa.
 Let's build it just like when you were
   a little boy."
 Daddy answers every year,
 "Not this year, Ruth.
   Maybe next year, when David
     and you are older."

But this year,
    for this Sukkot,
        for the very first time,
            we are building our own *Sukkah*.

We use doors and old lumber
to make the walls.

There are many nails to hammer,
hinges to screw in the door.

We gather tree branches
and cut down corn stalks.
There's a lot of work to do.

We put the branches and cornstalks
across the tops of the walls.

We make a roof, a different kind of roof,
    a roof where the stars and the moon
        shine through for all the days of Sukkot.
We are making a little house,   a Sukkot hut
    for our family and our friends.

We hang up strings of cranberries
    and yellow ears of corn.
We hang up squashes, green peppers,
    purple bunches of grapes.

We carry in a table.
We set six chairs around.

Mother spreads a clean white cloth
across our *Sukkah* table.
Apples and pears and plums in a bowl,
in the middle of the clean white cloth.

David carries out the candlesticks.
I carry out dishes and glasses.
David carries out napkins and silver.

We set our Sukkot table
>   for our first Sukkot dinner.
Grandma and Grandpa sit at our table.

Grandpa says to Daddy,
>   "Remember our *Sukkah*?"
Grandma says to Mother,
>   "It's just like our *Sukkah*."
Mother says,
>   "The children always wanted
>   our very own *Sukkah*,
>   just like their Daddy's,
>   to eat in the whole holiday."

We eat our dinner in our very own *Sukkah*.
The candles are burning on the table.
The moon and the stars are shining
>   through the roof.
Mother makes good food to eat
>   in our first *Sukkah*.

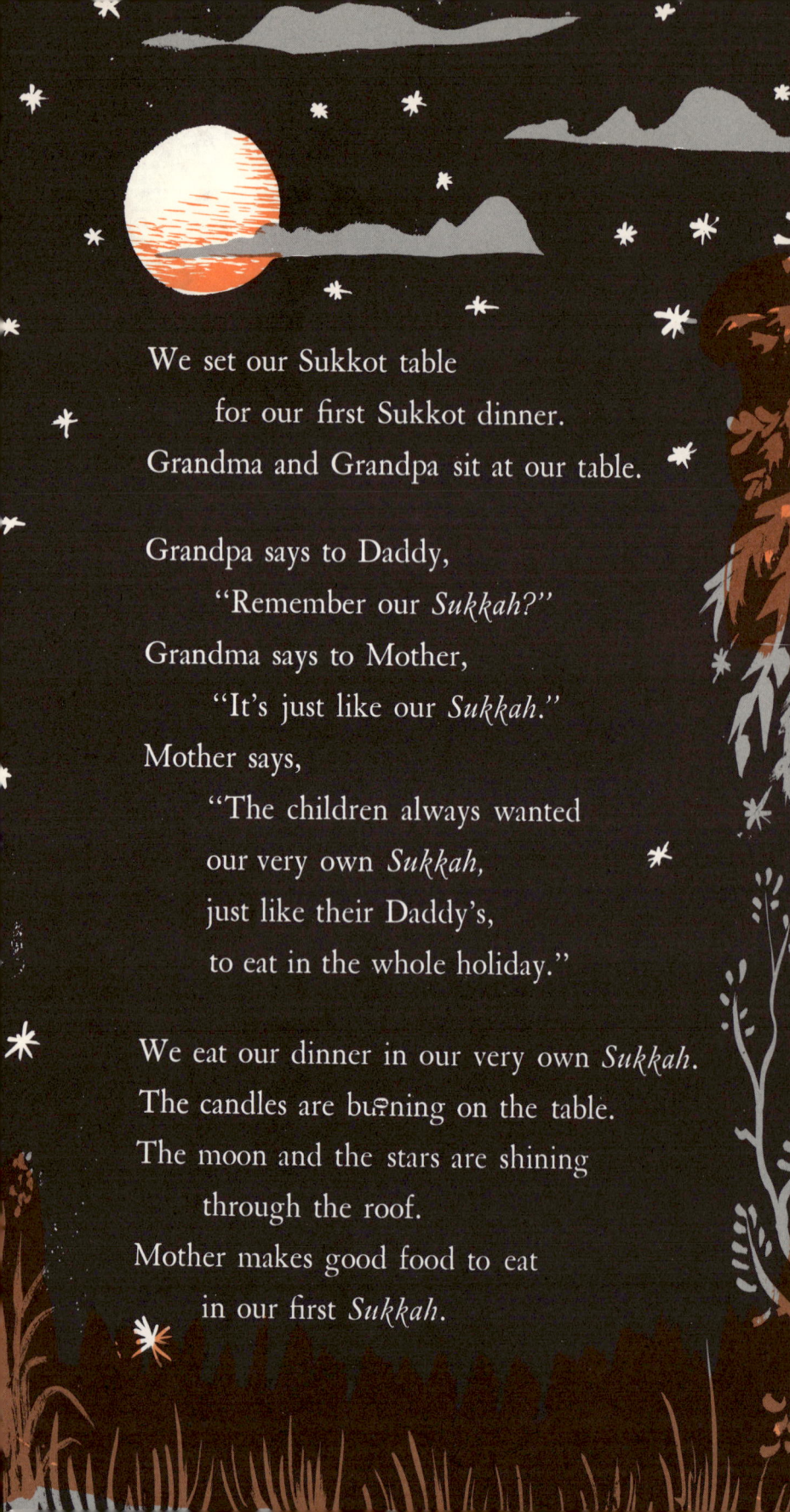

Our friends come to sit in our *Sukkah*.
We carry out benches and chairs.
We sit around the table.
We all begin to sing.
The grownups drink wine.
The children crack nuts.
We sing, we drink, we eat, we laugh,
in our first *Sukkah*.

One night it rains right through our roof and makes our table wet. We can't eat in our *Sukkah* until a drier day.

But most of the days,
    the many days of Sukkot,
    the sun shines through our roof all day,
    and the moon and the stars
    shine through at night.

We eat breakfast, lunch, and dinner
 in our very own *Sukkah*.
Our *Sukkah* is just like Daddy's
 when he was a little boy,
 and this year we made it ourselves.